Busy Boats

A Random House PICTUREBACK®

PETER LIPPMAN

Busy

Boats

Random House
New York

Long ago, explorers and merchants crossed the ocean in great wooden sailing ships, searching for gold and spices. Often they spent months at sea, waiting for the wind to blow them to far-off shores. The lookout in the crow's-nest watched for land. . . . *Ahoy!*

Today, huge steel ships with powerful engines hurry from port to port. When a cargo ship docks in the harbor, its big booms and cranes quickly unload everything onto the dock—wild animals, ripe bananas, crates filled with goods from foreign lands. Trucks are lined up on the pier. They will carry the cargo to cities and towns far away from the water.

Tugboats are small, but their engines are big, and very powerful. They help big ships get in and out of the busy harbor. Tugboats can do many things that bigger boats can't do. In crowded harbors, huge freighters and ocean liners must turn down their engines and go slowly. Tugboats push and pull them along and keep them from bumping other boats until the big ships are out on the open sea.

An ocean liner carries hundreds of people on relaxing
vacation cruises. Special elevators take their cars down
to the hold. People use another elevator to get from deck
to deck. The baker and butcher, dentist and doctor,
nurses and hairdressers, chefs and waiters,
and the captain and his crew are busy
taking care of all those passengers.

QUEEN ANNE I

It is fun to take a cruise on one of these giant, floating hotels. On long trips you can even take your pets along. People watch plays and eat in restaurants and go to movies. They play games and swim in the pool on deck. At night they sleep in their own cabins. Far below, in the noisy engine room, the crew makes sure the ship is running smoothly.

Hydrofoils are very fast boats. They take passengers on short trips. Hydrofoils skim the top of the water on wing-like blades attached to the hull. As the boat speeds along, the "wings" lift it higher. The hull barely touches the water.

A large hovercraft can carry cars as well as passengers. Its big jet propellers suck in air above the boat and push it out below the boat. Rubber "skirts" hold the air below so that the hovercraft whooshes along on a cushion of air.

Some boats are busy even though they are standing still. This one is drilling for oil, deep in the ocean floor. Submarines help under water by exploring the ocean bottom with lights and television cameras. Other submarines have mechanical arms for picking up plants, rocks, wreckage—and, maybe, sunken treasure!

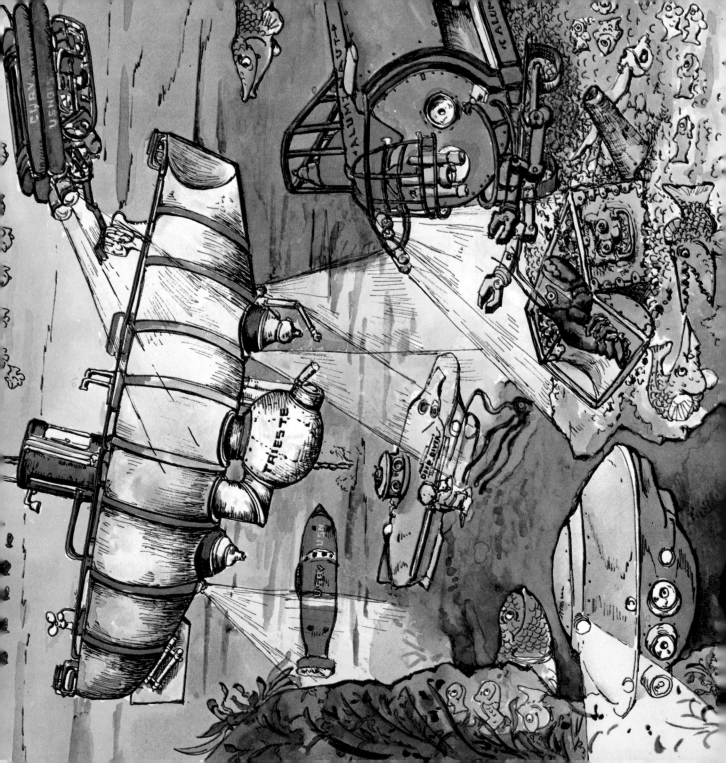

Floating cranes and derricks are built to lift very heavy loads.

They lift heavy cargo onto big ships and deliver supplies to oil-drilling platforms far from shore. They can even lift small submarines. When a floating crane picks up a load, tanks below deck take in tons of sea water to balance the crane so it won't tip over.

Sometimes there is an accident at sea. Then a Coast Guard cutter hurries to the rescue. This freighter has had an explosion on board. The Coast Guard crewmen are pulling people out of the water. The helicopter is bringing rescued sailors aboard the cutter.

410

The Coast Guard also helps when a giant supertanker springs a leak. Oil is spilling everywhere! The Coast Guard cutter and the tugboat are busy putting out rubber floats to keep the big black oil slick from spreading. "Slick lickers" suck up gallons of oil and pump it into barges. Busy boats keep the water clean and safe for animals and plants that live in the ocean.

★ TITANIC MERCHANT ★

When a ship catches fire in the harbor, fireboats rush in to put out the blaze. Even a tugboat can help with its big water gun. Some sailors are escaping from the burning cargo ship in a tiny fireproof lifeboat.

Sometimes busy boats need to sail where the sea is frozen. Then an icebreaker smashes through the thick ice. Snow and icebergs keep other big ships from getting through. *Crunch! Crash!* The icebreaker clears a path.

Fishermen in icy cold climates use Aleutian umiaks. They are small enough to find a way around big chunks of ice. Some umiaks even have outboard motors.

Many boats are used just for fun! Some people row, some paddle, and some pedal their boats. Others speed along through the water in motor boats. *Pull that water-skier away from the crowds!*

Watch out, swimmers! It is not safe to swim so close to all those busy boats!

There are people who use boats for houses—sometimes all year round and sometimes just for the summer. They cook and sleep on their houseboats. They can go for a swim whenever they want to. At night they may anchor far from shore, or stop over at a marina.

Boats can take the place of lighthouses. Lightships sail to danger spots where there are rocks, wrecks, or shallow water. Their bright lights flash warnings to the other boats: *Be careful here! Land is near!* Captains steer their ships away from danger so that all busy boats can get safely home.